Better Homes

PATCHWORK PROJECTS

15 FULL-SIZE PATTERNS

First Edition. Third Printing, 1985.
ISBN: 0-696-02113-7

PATCHWORK FOR ALL SEASONS

Summer, fall, winter, spring—capture the special spirit of every season of the year with the patchwork projects shown here and on the following pages.

For starters, you'll be able to breeze through an entire year with these colorful, quick-to-make wind-sock banners embellished with familiar seasonal motifs. Make one and you're sure to want to stitch a few more to present to family and friends. Directions for all the projects begin on page 12.

SPRING

In springtime let your fancy turn to hearts and flowers with these sweet, simple-to-make valentine mementos. Bits of brightly colored felt, ribbon, and odds and ends of beads and lace are all you need to craft a heart for someone special. Or, make a basketful to share with friends and loved ones.

Plump the four-inch hearts with fiberfill to turn them into pincushions. For sweet bags, used in times past to lightly scent closets and drawers, fill the hearts with fragrant dried flowers and herbs—red roses for love, rosemary for remembrance, and a pinch of saffron for joy and laughter.

SUMMER

Simple lines and a minimum number of pieces make this goose pattern quick and easy to appliqué. The cook's apron, *left,* is sized to fit everyone in the family and is embellished with a sprightly goose designed to keep a watchful eye on your backyard barbecue.

Use the same pattern for the 12-inch-square table mat, *above,* or alter the lines of the back and tail slightly to make the 16-inch-square pillow. For all three porch and patio favorites, machine-appliqué the goose in place, then outline the wing and add the eye using zigzag stitches.

FALL

When the chill of fall is in the air, stitch some festive decorations like the cluster of autumn leaves gathered into a door swag, *right.* Similar leaves, stitched from scraps of calico, accent the handsome grapevine wreath, *opposite.*

Use a purchased wreath, or craft your own from vines gathered in your backyard or during a short walk in the woods.

The maple leaf quilt, *below,* pieced in the vibrant colors of autumn, is sure to spruce up a corner of your favorite room or a bed reserved for holiday guests.

Calico squares and solid-color triangles are joined together to make each of the 49 pieced blocks in this 81x99-inch quilt. (There are 50 plain blocks, too.) For a smaller quilt, stitch fewer blocks and join them into a lap-size throw.

WINTER

This quaint winter wonderland is reminiscent of traditional folk art painting. Its beauty lies in its simplicity—primitive, childlike shapes combine to make the charming overall design.

Using snippets of lace, ribbon, and fabric, you can assemble most of this 11x15½-inch winter scene on your sewing machine. Then add some hand-embroidered flourishes like the French knot snowflakes and the twigs on the trees.

To make this fabric painting truly personal, you might alter the design of the house to match your own (or that of a friend or loved one). Then, select fabrics, ribbons, and trims that suggest the colors and textures of the real house. You're sure to look forward every year to displaying the finished design with pleasure and pride.

WINTER

If your workbasket is full of odds and ends of fabrics left from previous projects, you won't have to purchase a thing to make the whimsical tree trims, *right.* Just machine-appliqué easy-sew fabrics to felt backings, add hand- and machine-embroidered details, and presto! You're all done.

The ornaments are so quick and easy to stitch that in no time you'll be able to embellish a wreath or a tabletop tree and still have a batch for your favorite bazaar.

Traditional Christmas colors and patchwork patterns symbolic of the holidays make the wall quilt, *opposite,* a splendid seasonal accent.

The large center block is pieced in the popular Christmas Lilies pattern. Side borders are strips of Trees Everlasting, and six Holly Berry Baskets trim the lower edge. Red and green borders finish this 32½x38½-inch design.

Wind Socks

Shown on pages 2 and 3.

Finished size is 53 inches high, and 10 inches in diameter.

MATERIALS

For one wind sock

Rip-stop nylon in 5 or 6 colors
32-inch length of fabric-covered dressmaker's boning
Typing paper
Transparent sewing thread
3 brass grommets
3 yards of nylon cord
1 barrel swivel

INSTRUCTIONS

From nylon, cut five 5x30-inch strips for the body of the sock and eight 5x30-inch strips for the tails. (Refer to the photograph for color suggestions.)

Using transparent thread and ¼-inch seams, stitch body strips together along long edges to form a large rectangle. To minimize puckering on slippery nylon, place strips of typing paper between the fabric and the throat plate on the sewing machine. Stitch, then tear away paper.

Referring to the photograph for ideas, trace seasonal shapes (shown here and on pages 13 and 14) and cut them out of leftover pieces of nylon. (Trace only the outline of the heart; use the remainder of the pattern for felt heart projects.) Machine zigzag-stitch appliqués in place randomly across striped assembly.

To make tails, fold under both long edges and one short edge of tailpieces ⅜ inch; fold under again and stitch. Next, align raw (top) edges of tailpieces, alternating colors as desired.

To assemble the wind sock, sew top edges of tails to bottom edge of body, right sides facing. Reinforce seam by zigzag-stitching along raw edges, close to seam. Sew short edges of sock together, right sides facing, to form tube. Zigzag-stitch along raw edges.

Using a zipper foot, stitch right side of boning to right side of sock at top. Turn boning to inside; stitch close to boning.

Place three grommets evenly spaced along top edge, just beneath boning casing.

Cut cord into three 1-yard lengths. Fold one cord in half. Thread through one grommet; pull two ends through folded loop to secure. Repeat with other cords. Fasten ends of cord to barrel swivel; melt nylon cords with a lighted match to secure ends.

Hang sock from barrel swivel.

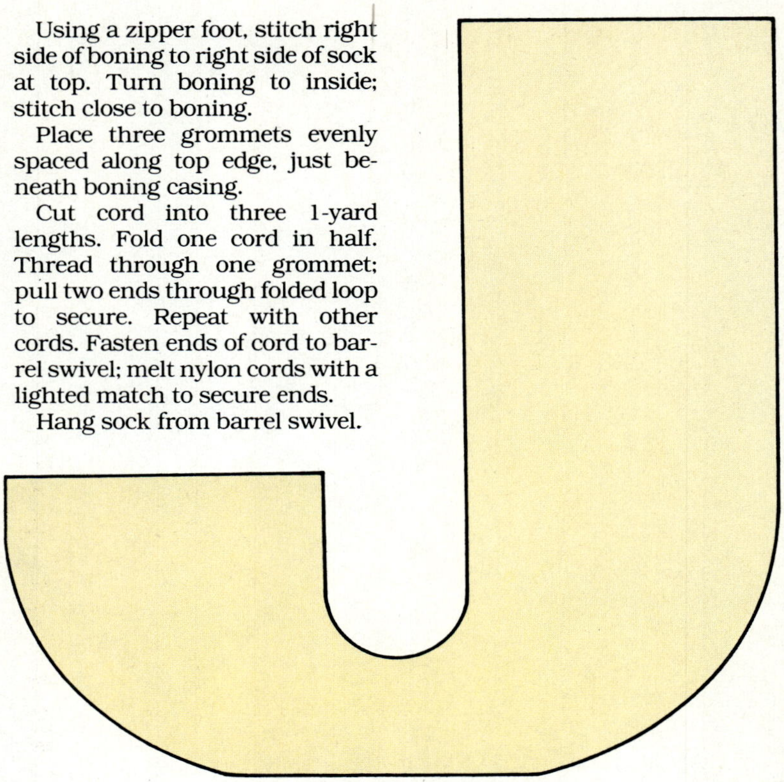

Felt Hearts

Shown on page 4.

MATERIALS
Felt scraps in assorted colors
Fiberfill or potpourri
Narrow lace edging
Small beads
Fabric glue

INSTRUCTIONS

Using the photograph as a color guide, trace the larger heart shape, *left,* onto paper and transfer to felt; cut front and back pieces. Baste lace ⅛ inch from edge of heart front.

With right sides facing, stitch heart front to back. Leave a small opening for turning. Clip curves, turn right side out, and stuff firmly with fiberfill or potpourri, as desired. Sew the opening closed.

Trace the smaller heart and cut it from felt in a contrasting color. Glue (or stitch) the heart to the front of the ornament. Next, cut felt flowers in a variety of colors; also cut out leaves. Glue or tack leaves and flowers to the small heart as shown in the diagram; add beads for flower centers. Attach ribbon loop for hanging.

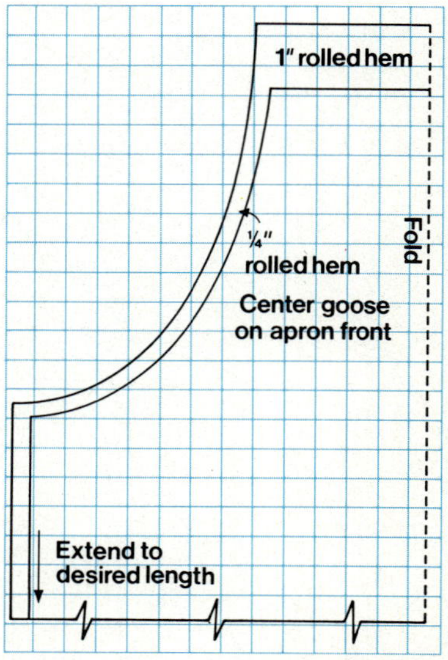

1 square = 1 inch

Goose Table Mat, Pillow, and Apron

Shown on page 5.

MATERIALS

1½ yards of print fabric for apron and pillow; ⅓ yard of fabric for table mat
White and yellow cotton fabrics for appliqués
Iron-on interfacing (optional)
1-inch D rings for apron
Fiberfill for pillow; batting for table mat

INSTRUCTIONS

For table mat: Cut front, back, and batting 12½ inches square. Layer batting, backing, and top; stitch, leaving an opening. Turn; sew opening. Using pattern, page 15, cut beak and bird from appliqué fabrics and interfacing (do not add seam allowances). Iron interfacing to wrong side of appliqués. Zigzag-stitch appliqués to front. Zigzag-stitch eye and wing.

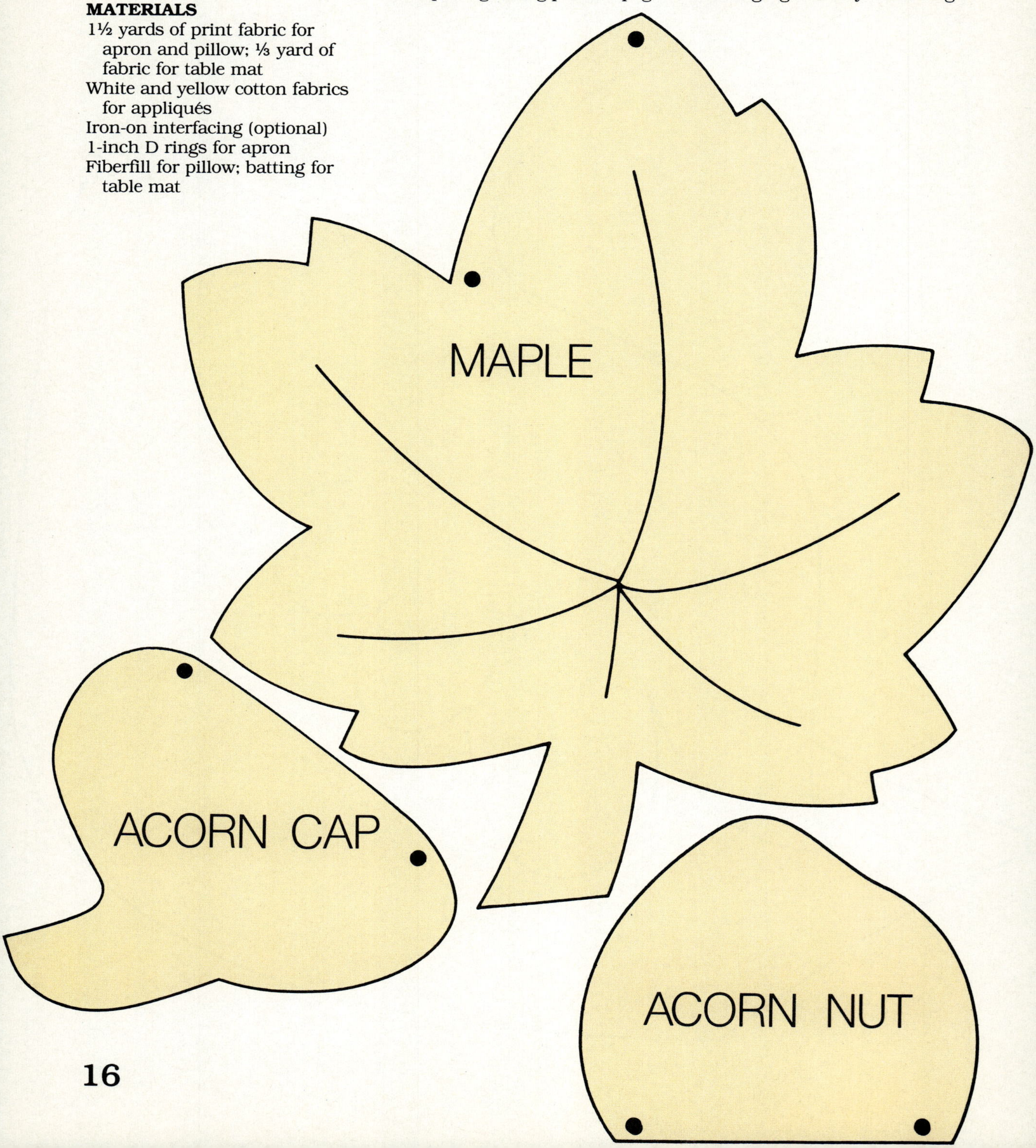

For pillow: Cut back and front, each 16½ inches square. Trace pattern; reshape if desired, using photograph as a guide. Following directions above, appliqué bird and beak to pillow front. Sew pillow front to back, turn, and stuff.

For apron: Enlarge apron pattern, page 14; transfer to fabric. Cut apron and three 3x30-inch strips. Fold long edges of strips to center; fold again and stitch through all layers along folded edge and across one end. Cut one finished strip into two pieces—6 inches long and 24 inches long.

Narrowly hem apron edges; insert 6-inch strap folded with D rings and 24-inch strap at top corners. Add apron ties to each side. Stitch appliqués to bib.

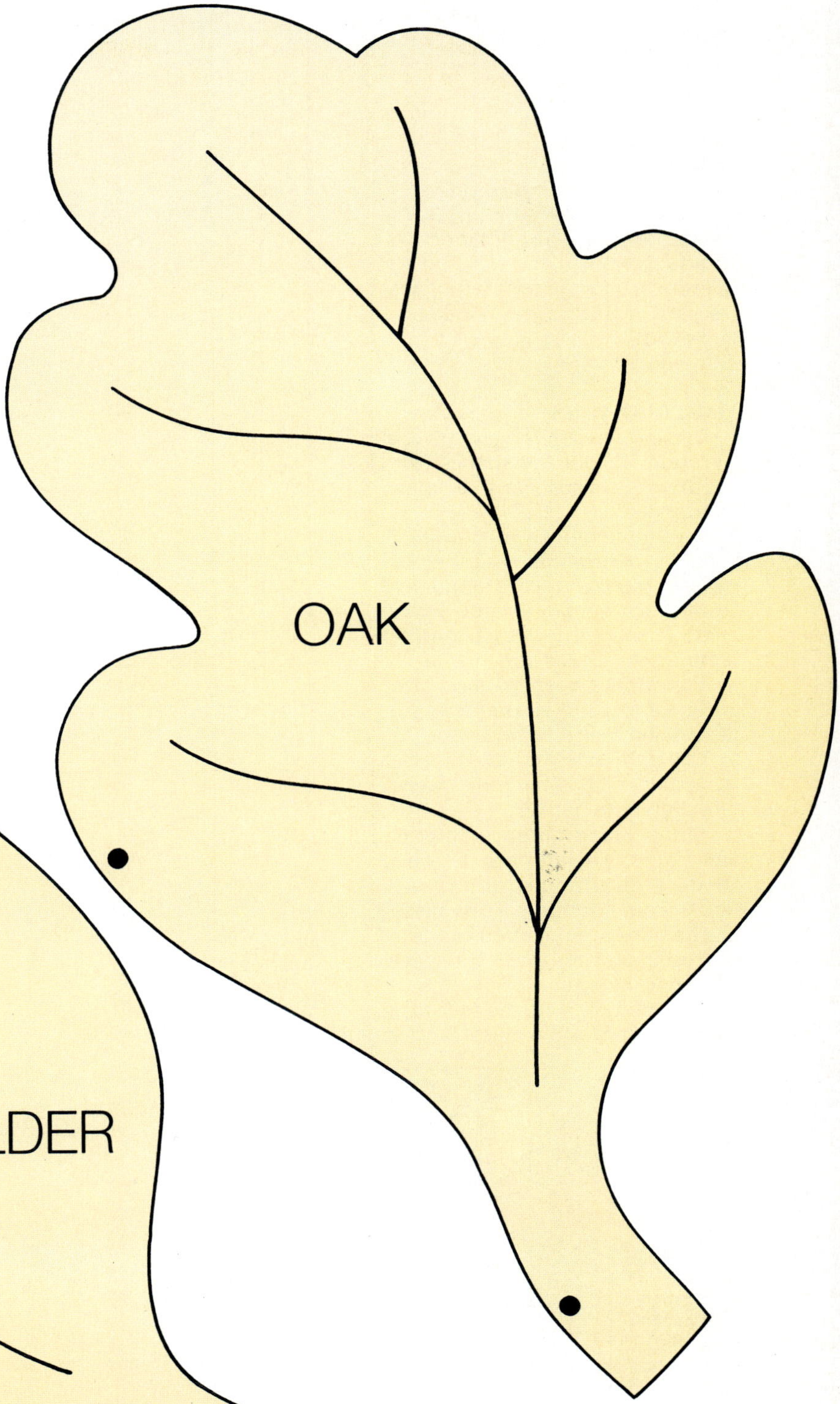

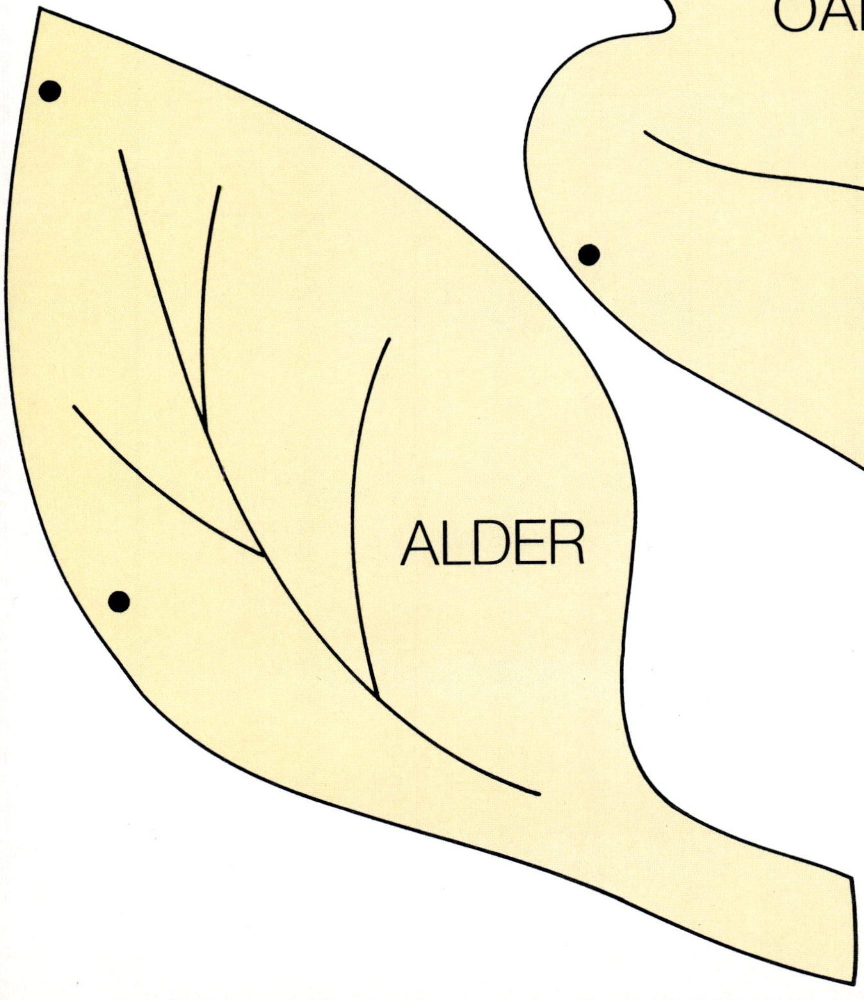

Autumn Leaves Wreath

Shown on page 6.

MATERIALS

Grapevine wreath
¼ yard each of 6 calico prints (fabrics A through F), plus an additional ¼ yard of fabrics A and B
Cardboard for pattern templates
¼ yard of thick, firm, bonded batting
Fine florist wire

INSTRUCTIONS

Trace patterns, pages 16 and 17, and cut out the shapes from lightweight cardboard to make templates.

Designate fabrics A through F. Leaving approximately 1 inch between pieces, trace around leaf and acorn templates onto *wrong* side of fabrics indicated on diagrams. *Do not cut out.*

For variety, turn pattern piece over for tracing second leaf; finished shape will be reversed.

Lay right sides of traced fabrics together with matching fabric. Pin lightly to batting.

Stitch along outlines through all layers, leaving open between dots. Trim through all layers ¼ inch from stitching. Turn pieces right side out and stitch closed.

Topstitch vein lines. Hand-sew acorn cap to nut.

For the bow, cut the following shapes from both A and B fabrics:

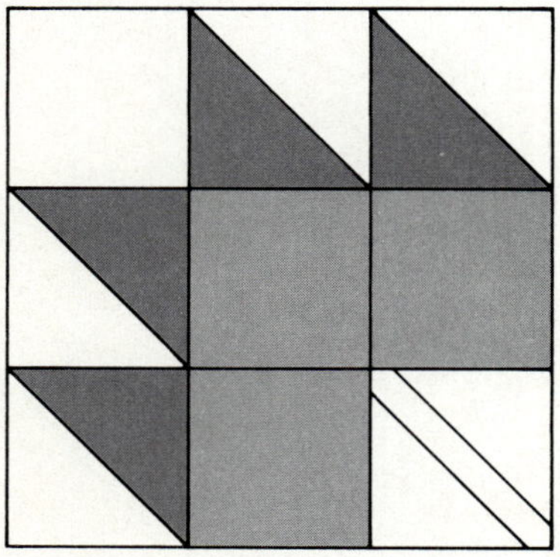

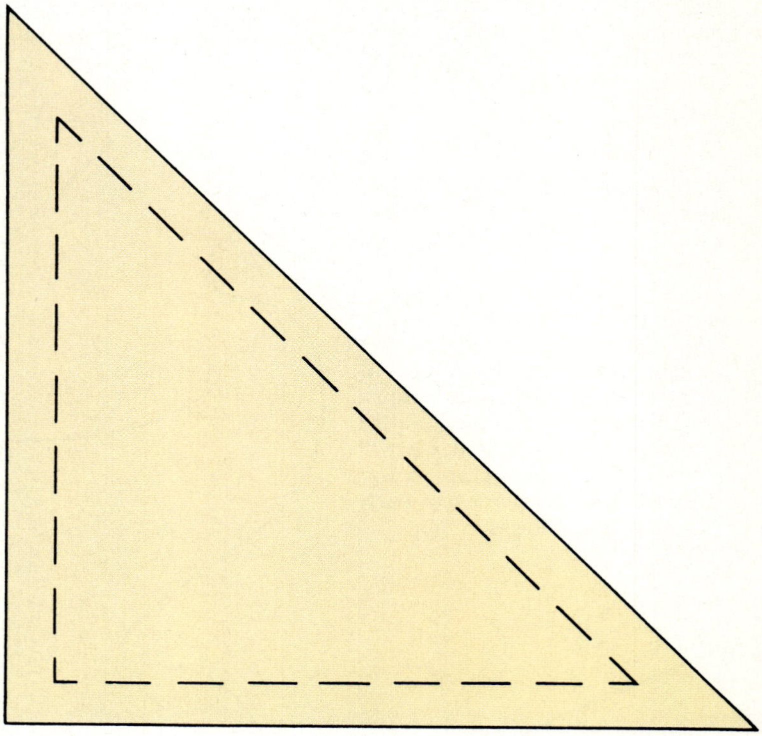

a 4x16-inch rectangle (loops), a 4x4-inch square (knot), and two 4x8-inch rectangles (tails). Using one piece of each fabric, stitch together, right sides facing; leave one end open for turning. Turn, press, and stitch closed.

Hand-stitch short ends of loop piece together; wrap knot piece around center and tack in back. Pleat top edge of tailpieces and tack to back of bow.

Arrange leaves on wreath (see photograph), and wire in place with florist wire. Add bow.

Leaf Door Swag

Shown on page 7.

MATERIALS

⅓ yard each of four autumn-color calico fabrics
⅓ yard of firm, bonded batting
Five 18-inch lengths of grosgrain ribbon; 5 brass bells
1 curtain ring

INSTRUCTIONS

Trace leaf patterns, pages 16 and 17. Select three fabrics for leaves and one for bow. Draw around leaves onto wrong side of each fabric. *Do not cut out.*

Place traced fabric atop backing fabric (right sides facing); place both layers atop batting. Stitch through all three layers, leaving open between dots. Trim seam allowance to ¼ inch. Clip curves, trim corners, and turn. Sew opening closed. Topstitch vein lines.

For bow, cut a 6x45-inch rectangle. Fold in half lengthwise and sew raw edges together, making diagonal points on each end and leaving an opening for turning. Turn, press, and stitch closed.

Layer leaves (spread apart slightly) with the largest on the bottom and the smallest on top. Tack together. Tack bells to ends of ribbon. Arrange at staggered lengths; tack in place.

Tie bow around stems. Stitch curtain ring to back for hanging.

Maple Leaf Quilt

Shown on page 7.

MATERIALS

Scraps of green, red, yellow, gold, rust, and brown solid and print fabrics
7 yards of white fabric (44 or 45 inches wide) for plain blocks
6 yards of muslin (44 or 45 inches wide) for backing
Quilt batting
Cardboard or plastic for pattern templates
12 yards of green pindot double-fold bias tape

INSTRUCTIONS

This quilt is made from ninety-nine 9-inch-square blocks (finished dimensions). Use ¼-inch seam allowances throughout.

Trace triangle and square patterns, *opposite,* then cut out templates. (Solid line is cutting line; broken line is seam line.)

Cut 50 plain white blocks, each 9½x9½ inches. Set aside.

For each pieced block cut two white squares, four white triangles, three print squares, and four coordinating solid-color triangles. Sew white triangles to colored triangles to make 3½-inch-square patches. Using the diagram of the quilt block, *opposite,* as a guide, sew the block together.

Turning under raw edges, appliqué a narrow strip of green fabric diagonally across the lower right square for a stem. Make 49 pieced blocks.

To assemble the top, lay out quilt blocks, alternating pieced and plain blocks, in nine rows of 11 blocks each. Stitch blocks into rows, then sew rows together.

Cut quilt batting 2 inches larger all around than pieced top. Piece and cut a muslin backing to match batting. Sandwich batting between top and backing; baste. Outline-quilt around each piece, or in the pattern of your choice.

Trim batting and backing and finish edges with bias tape.

Winter Scene

Shown on pages 8 and 9.

MATERIALS

6x18 inches of blue cotton (sky)
6x15½ inches *each* of white cotton and white lace (snow)
Scraps of red and green polka-dot fabrics
7 inches *each* of brown, dark brown, and gray ⅜-inch-wide grosgrain ribbons
1 yard *each* of gray and brown ⅛-inch-wide grosgrain ribbons
Ribbon scraps for windows, chimney, and house foundation
Brown, gray, and white embroidery floss
11x15½ inches *each* of cotton backing and quilt batting
Wide red and white bias tape
5 inches of ½-inch-wide blue ribbon (walkway); cotton (smoke)

INSTRUCTIONS

Trace pattern, page 20, onto tissue and cut apart. Cut sky, house, roof, and four pine trees from fabrics, adding ¼-inch seam allowances. See photograph for colors.

Machine-appliqué house, roof, and two pine trees to sky. Stitch brown ribbon tree trunks under pine trees. Hand-sew the narrow brown ribbon in tree branch formation; add ⅜-inch-wide brown ribbon tree trunks. Finish house details with ribbon scraps.

Next, sew ribbon walkway atop center of white cotton. Lay lace over white cotton; sew in place. Turn under top edge of snow; appliqué to sky, matching walkway to door. Appliqué remaining trees on snow.

Machine-embroider fence along dotted lines; hand-embroider twigs on tree branches. Make falling snow with white floss French knots; sew cotton to chimney.

Layer top, batting, and backing. Machine-baste around the outer edge; bind edge with wide bias tape. Frame as desired.

Holiday Wall Quilt

Shown on page 11.

MATERIALS

1¼ yards *each* of dark green and ecru cotton fabrics
1 yard of red and green print on ecru background (for tree-trunk strips and lily blocks)
½ yard *each* red and white print and red pindot fabrics
⅛ yard solid-red fabric
1 yard of backing fabric
35x42 inches of quilt batting
Plastic for templates
Water-erasable transfer pen

INSTRUCTIONS

To make templates: Trace the patterns for the Christmas Lilies block, *below,* and the Holly Berry Basket, page 22. To make piecing easier, on each pattern piece note the name of the pattern.

Without adding seam allowances, cut templates for the pattern shapes. Note the name of the pattern on each template (or on paper taped to the template).

For the Christmas Lilies block, also draw two 4-inch squares; cut one 4-inch-square plastic template for the plain squares in the design. Cut the second 4-inch square in half diagonally, making two triangles; cut a plastic template for one triangle. Do not add seam allowances to these pieces.

For berries in Holly Berry Basket, draw and cut a template in the shape of 1-inch-diameter circle. Do not add seam allowances.

To make a template for Trees Everlasting, draw a rectangle 2x3 inches; divide the rectangle diagonally, making two elongated triangles. Without adding seam allowances, cut a template for one of the triangles.

To cut fabrics: Using the fabrics indicated below, trace around templates onto the *wrong* side of the fabric, using a water-erasable pen; these are the stitching lines. Cut out the pieces ¼ inch beyond the marked lines and use ¼-inch seams throughout. After stitching, press seams to one side.

For Holly Berry Baskets: Cut pieces from ecru, solid-red (berries), red pindot, and red and white print fabrics (see photograph). Appliqué the handle and three holly berries to large ecru triangle. (For the handle, cut a bias strip 1 inch wide; turn under edges and sew in place, easing around the curve.)

Piece the remaining basket and background pieces to form a 6-inch block. Make six blocks. Piece blocks into a horizontal strip.

For Trees Everlasting: Using template, cut 32 ecru patches and 32 dark green patches.

Piece ecru and dark green triangles into rectangles, making 32 (16 for each border strip). See photograph for position of lights and darks within each strip.

Join eight rectangles along the short sides, making four strips. Next, cut a red and green print strip 2¾x26 inches (trim excess length later). (Finished width of this strip is 2¼ inches.)

Stitch this tree-trunk strip between two strips of rectangles (bough strips). Set aside.

Position side strips along top and sides of lower border (Berry Basket strip). Baste but do not sew together. The resulting opening is for the Christmas Lilies block. Carefully measure dimensions of opening; draw on paper.

For Christmas Lilies: From dark green fabric, cut one large (4-inch) square, four half-square triangles, and four smaller triangles for the base of the lily block (see the photograph). From the ecru fabric, cut two 4-inch squares and seven half-square triangles. From the red and green print on ecru fabric, cut seven half-square

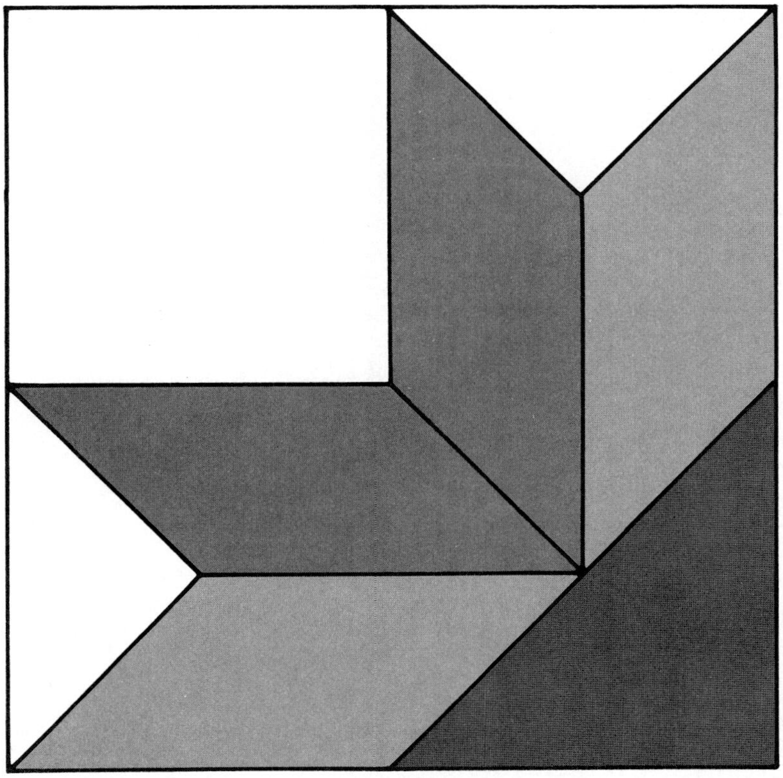

triangles, four lily-block squares and four lily-block small triangles. Cut eight diamond shapes *each* from red and white print and red pindot fabrics.

Assemble half-square triangles into squares: two with dark green and ecru fabrics; two with dark green and red and green print on ecru; and five with ecru and red and green print on ecru. Including solid squares, you will have 12 squares for the center block.

For the four remaining pieced lily blocks, arrange four diamonds (petals) for each block; assemble according to the pattern.

To assemble center block, refer to photograph, arrange squares as shown, and sew them together.

Next, cut dark green fabric into 1-inch-wide strips. Sew strips to the center block, using ¼-inch seams, and mitering corners.

Turn under the seam allowance on the green border around the center block; press. Position center block atop paper drawing of square opening allowed for the Christmas Lilies block.

Carefully mark the dimensions of the triangles needed to border the center block (approximately 12x12x17 inches). Adjust measurements as necessary, so center block fits opening between pieced borders. Add seam margins to triangles, cut from ecru, and sew to sides of center block.

To assemble wall hanging: Sew Trees Everlasting strips to sides of center block; add bottom strip.

Trim edges with a ¾-inch-wide dark red strip (finished dimension is ¼ inch wide) and a 2½-inch-wide dark green strip; miter corners. Cut backing and batting to match top. Layer, baste, and quilt as desired. Trim 1 inch from batting and backing, turn green border to back; stitch.

Appliquéd Tree Trims

Shown on page 10.

MATERIALS

Green, red, and white felt
Scraps of brown, red, and rust pindot fabrics; red and white candy-stripe fabric; green print fabric; and medium green, dark green, blue, black, white, red, and peach solid-color fabrics
White, dark blue, brown, green, red, orange, and pink thread
Embroidery floss, fusible webbing
Pearl cotton for hanging loops

INSTRUCTIONS

Trace the patterns below and on page 24. Solid lines on the patterns indicate shapes to be cut from fabric and fused to felt backing; dotted lines indicate topstitched detail lines. To make the cutting patterns, first trace around overall shapes on tracing paper. Then draw around individual shapes on patterns such as scarf, bow, hat, heart, nose, heel, toe, candy cane, elf, and package shapes. Cut pieces apart to use as patterns. If you are planning to stitch more than just a few of these ornaments, you may wish to cut cardboard or plastic templates for the pieces.

Using the photograph as a color reference, cut shapes from assorted fabrics and fusible webbing.

Place the appliqué shapes, with webbing underneath, atop green felt background. Fuse with iron. (Protect iron from stray wisps of webbing by placing a paper towel between iron and fabrics. Follow instructions for fusing on webbing manufacturer's label.)

With your sewing machine set for closely spaced ⅛-inch-wide satin stitches, appliqué all shapes to green felt along all raw edges. (See photograph for thread colors.) Then, stitch along detail lines (dotted lines on patterns).

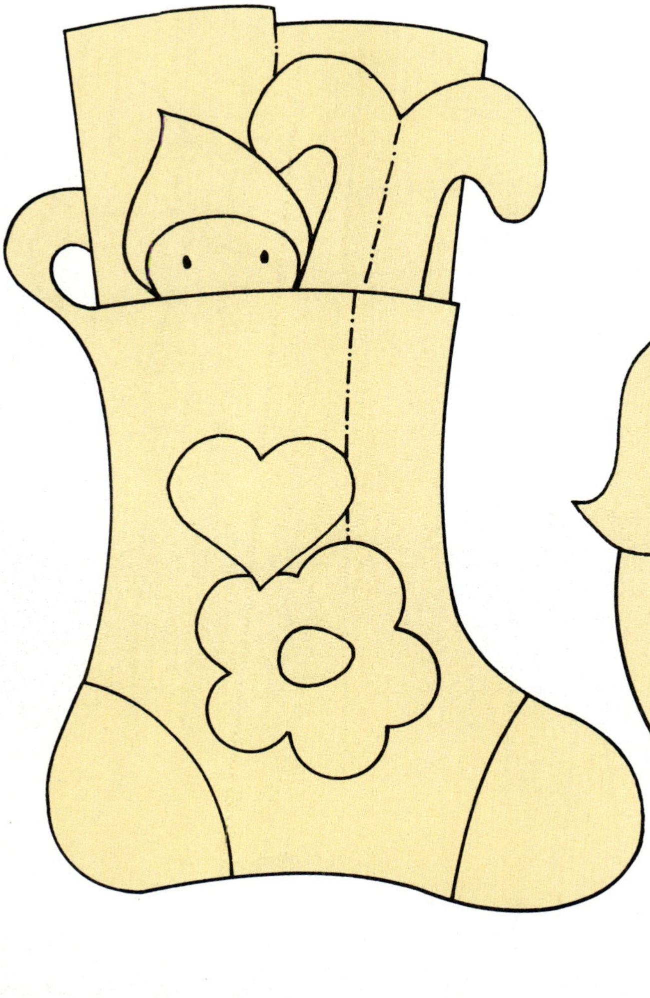

Add French knot eyes on all designs except the cat; embroider the cat's eyes with satin stitches worked by hand or machine.

Cut the ornaments away from the felt, leaving a ⅛-inch-wide border of felt all around.

For hanging loops, cut pearl cotton thread into 5-inch lengths. Stitch through tops of ornaments and knot ends together.

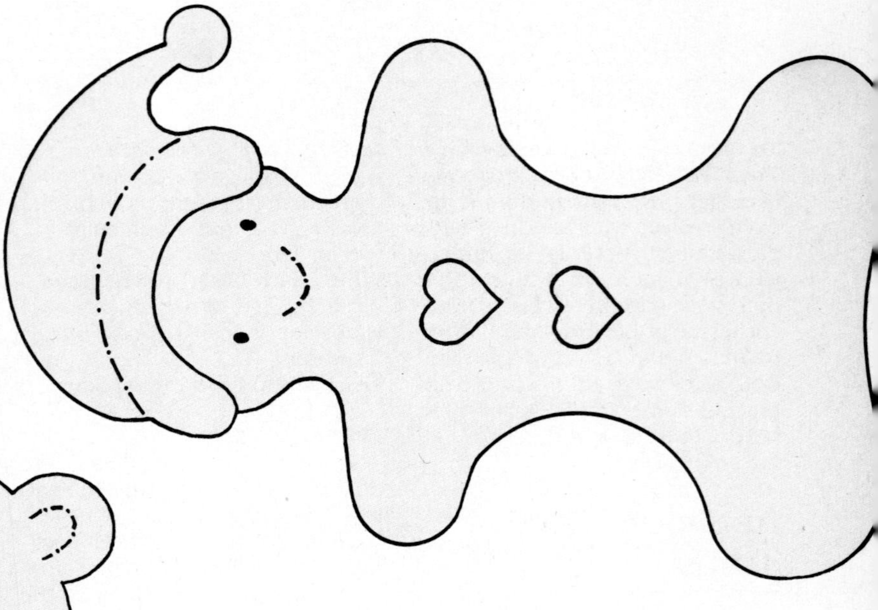

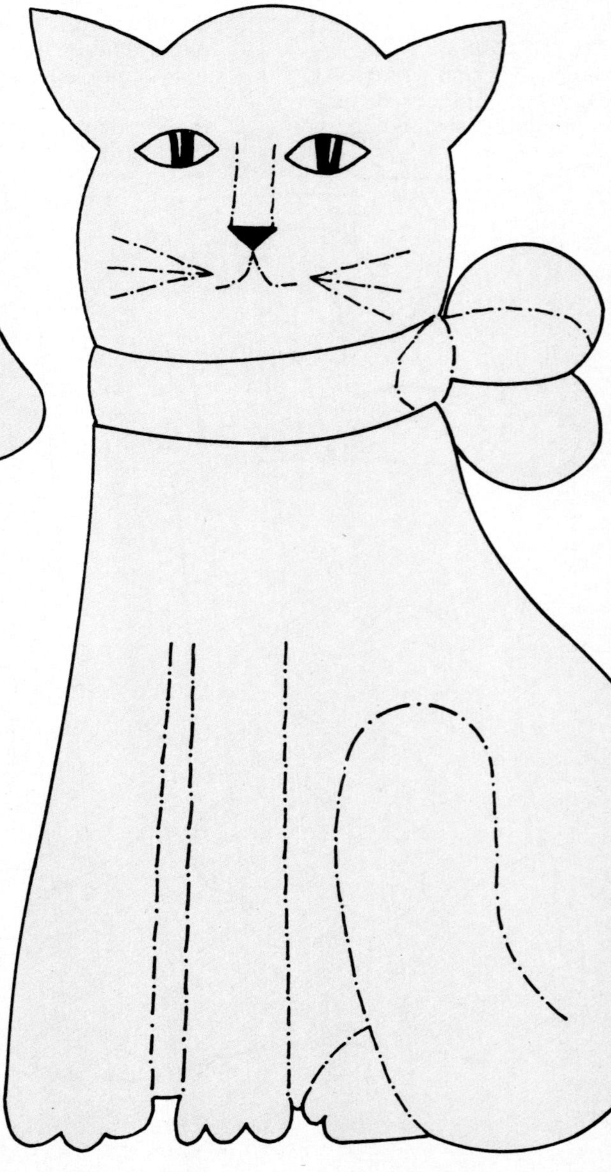